Panorama of the Hudson, Showing Both Sides of the River From New York to Albany as Seen From the Deck of the Hudson River day Line Steamers ... one Hundred and Fifty Miles of Continuous Scenery Accurately Represented From Eight Hundred Consecutive Photogr

NEW EDITION

PRICE ONE DOLLAR

SOLD ON HUDSON RIVER DAY LINE STEAMERS FOR 50 CENTS

BRYANT UNION PUBLISHING CO.

81 FULTON STREET

NEW YORK

r THE A. V. HAIGHT COMPANY

SENT POSTPAID ON REC

PANORAMA OF THE HUDSON

SHOWING BOTH SIDES OF THE RIVER FROM NEW YORK TO ALBANY

AS SEEN FROM THE DECK OF THE HUDSON RIVER DAY LINE STEAMERS

FIRST PHOTO-PANORAMA OF ANY RIVER EVER PUBLISHED

ONE HUNDRED AND FIFTY MILES OF CONTINUOUS SCENERY ACCURATELY REPRESENTED FROM EIGHT HUNDRED CONSECUTIVE PHOTOGRAPHS

FROM THE CAPITOL TO THE METROPOLIS THE HUDSON VARIES IN WIDTH FROM A HALF MILE TO FOUR MILES AND A HALF; BUT THE RIVER REMAINS UNIFORM IN THESE PAGES AS MOST CONVENIENT FOR A BOOK OF REFERENCE OR TOURIST GUIDE

STATUE OF LIBERTY
COMMUNIPAW
BROOKLYN BRIDGE
GOVERNOR'S ISLAND
BATTERY

LEHIGH VALLEY R. R.

P.

ST. PAUL'S

PENNA. R. R. FERRY

ERIE RAILROAD STATION
DEL. LACK. & WE
FALL RIVER LINE.
PENNA. R. R. FERRY
PEOPLE'S LINE.
CITY HALL SQU
DESBROSSES ST. NEW YORK AND ALBANY DAY LINE

[L]ACKAWANNA AND WESTERN

STEAMSHIP PIERS.

TWO MILES FROM BATTERY.

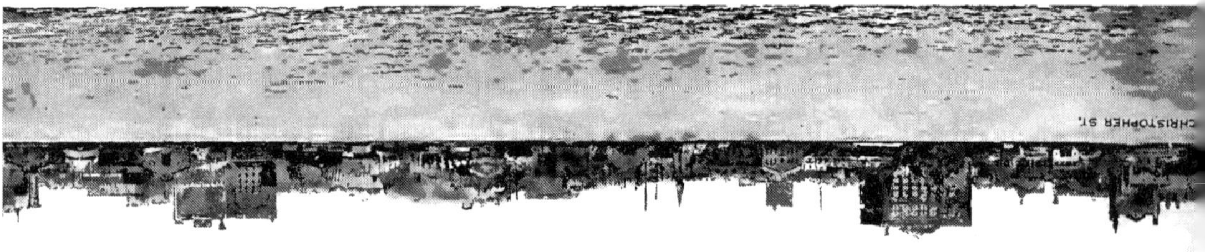

CASTLE POINT.

PIER 50.

ELYSIAN FIELDS

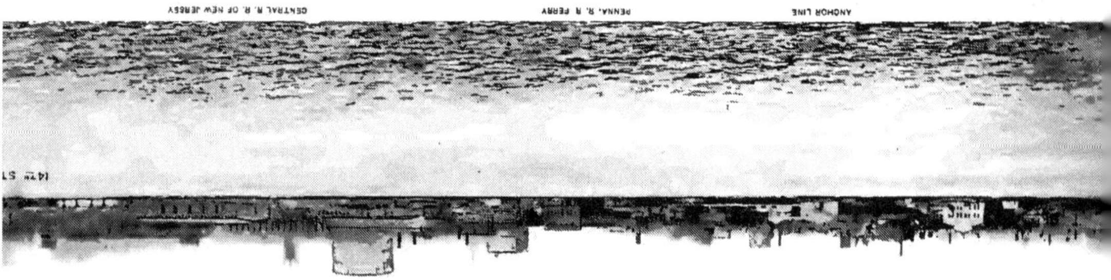
ANCHOR LINE
PENNA. R. R. FERRY
CENTRAL R. R. OF NEW JERSEY
14TH ST

FOUR MILES FROM BATTERY

ERIE R. R. PIERS. WESTSHORE AND N.Y. ONTARIO & WESTERN PASS

6 MILES FROM BATTERY.

WEST SHORE R.R.
WEST SHORE R.R.
WEST SHORE DOCKS & STATION
WEST SHORE ELEVATOR.

RIVERSIDE DRIVE

WEEHAWKEN

SOLDIER'S & SAILORS MONUMENT
RIVERSIDE DRIVE

EDGEWATER

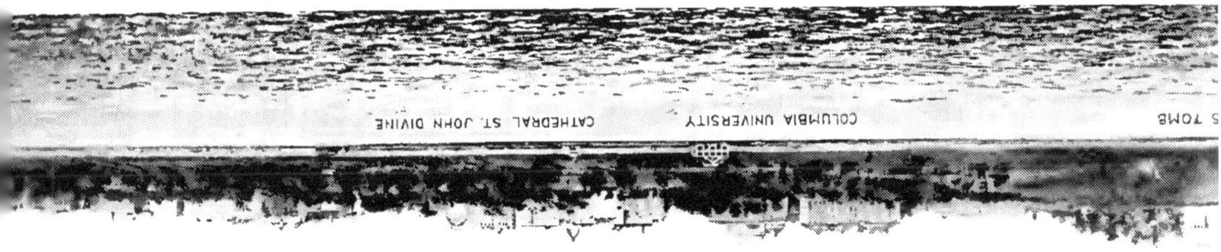
TOMB
COLUMBIA UNIVERSITY
CATHEDRAL ST. JOHN DIVINE

UNDERCLIFF

HEBREW ORPHAN ASYLUM
VIADUCT
129TH ST PIER N.Y. & ALE

FORT LEE HOTEL
SITE OF OLD FORT LEE

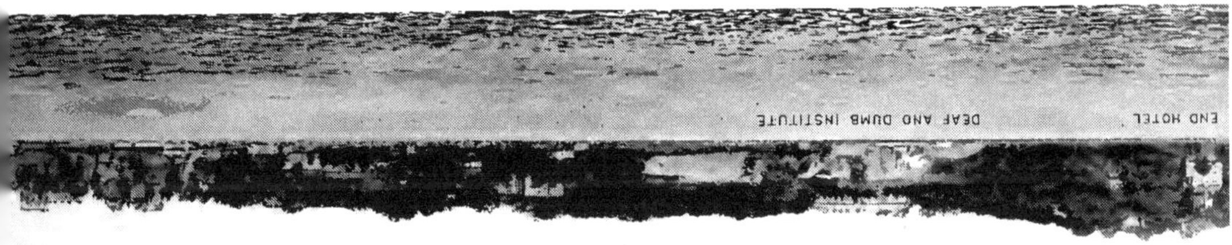
DEAF AND DUMB INSTITUTE
END HOTEL

PALISADES

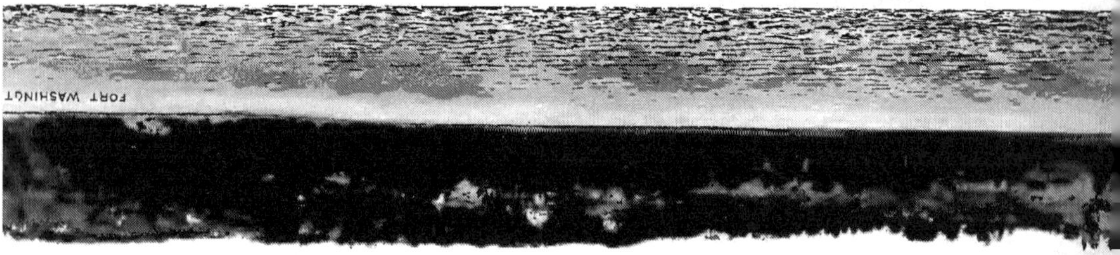
FORT WASHINGT

UNIVERSITY OF CITY OF NEW YORK

PALISADES

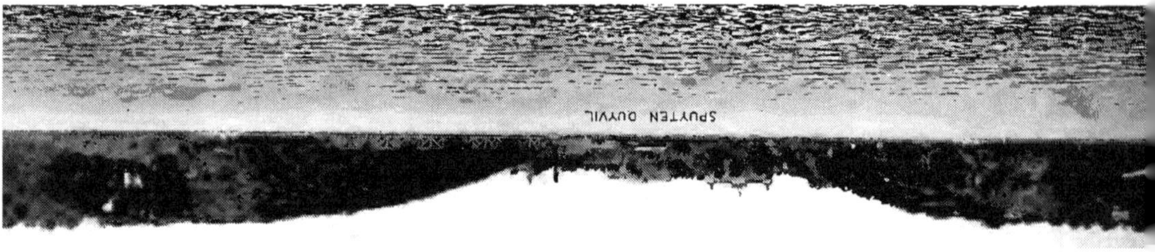
SPUYTEN DUYVIL

PALISADES

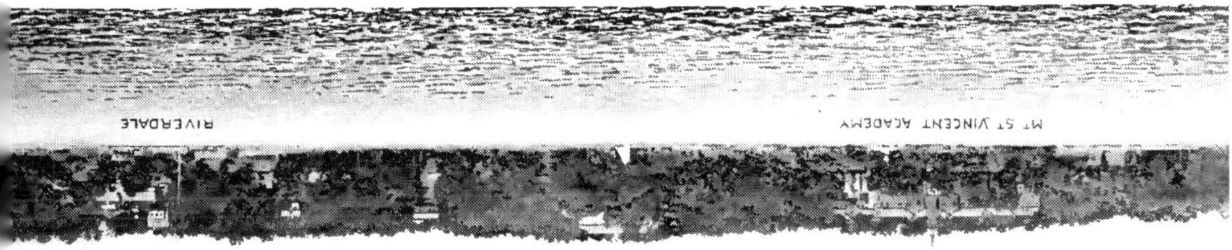
MT ST VINCENT ACADEMY
RIVERDALE

PALISADES

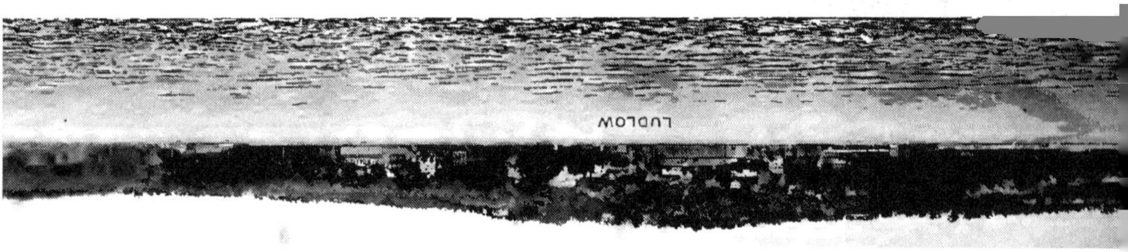
LUDLOW

PALISADES

N.Y. AND ALBANY DAY LINE
YONKERS

PALISADES

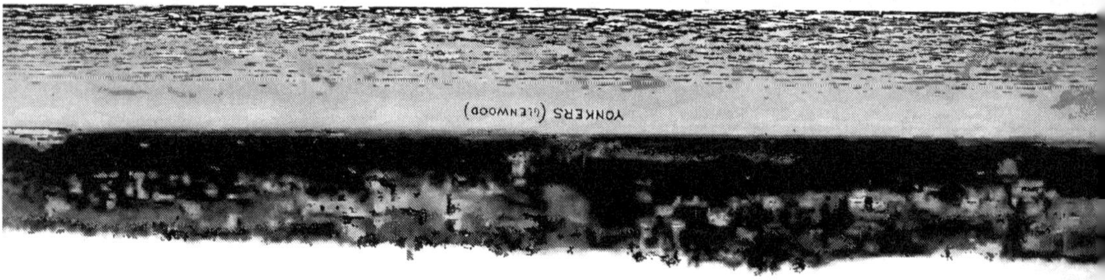
YONKERS (GLENWOOD)

PALISADES

"GREYSTONE," RESIDENCE OF THE LATE
HASTINGS

and a railway to the garden.

Tomb od General Ulysses S. Grant, on east bank at Riverside Park.

Manhattanville, above Riverside on east bank.

Edgewater, on west bank opposite Manhattanville

Trinity Cemetery, on east bank above Manhatt...

Fort Lee, on east bank; large Picnic Houses at foot of bluff.

Washington Heights and Fort Washington Point, on east bank, almost opposite Fort Lee.

Palisades, on west bank, extend fifteen miles from Fort lee to Piermort, a sheer wall of trap-rock from 300 to 500 feet high.

Spuyten Duyvil Xreek, on east bank, northern boundary of Manhattan Island.

Site of Fort Independence, east bank, on height above Spuyten Duyvil.

Riverdale Station, east bank, one mile and a half above Spuyten Duyvil.

Convent of Mount St. Vincent. The Castle like structure in front was once the home of Edwin Forrest, the Tragedian.

Yonkers, seventeen miles from Battery, on E. bar

Glenwood, north of Yonkers, E side. The fine residence near the river bank are J.B. Colgate's and J.B. Trevor's.

S.H. Lilienthal's Residence, on the E side, large building on ridge with tower, half mile from the river.

Mr. Schuyler's.

Irvington, 24 miles from New York.

Shady Nest, owned by Mrs. E. Phillips, on W bank just north of Erie Pier.

Tappan Zee, a great bay or inland lake of the Hudson, 10 miles long and in some places 3 miles wide, reaching from Dobbs Ferry to Croton Point.

Piermont, 24 miles from N.Y. on the W side. Pier almost 1 mile long extends into the Hud.

Sunnyside, E bank, hardly visible through the trees close to the River, about a half mile N of Irvington Station.

Residence of the late Jay Gould, known as "Lyndehurst," once known as the Paulding Manor House.

Cunningham Castle, with pointed tower on the hill; Bierstadt's residence (S of it), in ruins; the elegant house with pagodalike tower, recently built by Mr. Sigafuss; the spiral lock-cut tower of Robert Graves; Hatch Castle, embowered in trees on the hillside; and the new residences of Mr. Casey, Mr. Millard, and Mr. Andrews complete the picture on the eastern bank.

Tarrytown, E bank, 26 miles from New York, one of the historic and poetic towns of the Hudson

Nyack, W bank, opposite Tarrytown.

Rockwood, E bank, formerly the Aspinwall Estate. Owned by William Rockefeller. One of the most imposing residences on the Hudson.

the State Prison.

Rockland Lake, opposite Sing Sing, between 2 hills. This is the source of the Hackensack River, and a great Ice-quarry for New York.

Croton River, E bank, meets the Hudson one mile above Sing Sing, where we see the Drawbridge of the Hudson River Railroad.

Croton Point. Just above Croton River.

Teller's Point. That part of Croton Point which juts into the Hudson. This point separates Tappan Zee from Haverstraw Bay.

Haverstraw Bay, north of Teller's Point. Here the river is over 4 miles wide; the Mt. on the W side is High Torn.

The Shore R.R. here strikes the river. The view opened to the R.R. passenger, suddenly emerging from the tunnel, is striking and picturesque.

Haverstraw, on W side with 2 miles of brick-yds.

Stony Point, a mile above Grassy Point, W side.

Verplanck's Point, on E shore.

Tomkin's Cove, on W bank. Lime kilns & quarries

Seylmaker's Reach. A person looking N from this point sees no break in the mountains to mark the course of the river.

Peekskill, E ban , plesantly located.

N.Y. State Encampment, just N of Peekskill River.

Kidd's Point, now Caldwell's landing, on W side. The steamer turns this point almost at right angles and enters the Highlands.

the spot.
William H. Osborne's Residence. House with pointed tower, on the E bank of the river, just north of Sugar-Loaf.
Buttermilk Falls, near the river, on the E bank.
Hotel on the Bluff, known in early times as "Cozzen's Hotel."
West Point, 50 miles from N.Y. Academy, Parade, Grounds, etc.
Garrison. Opposite West Point, on E bank.
Kosciusko's Monument. W side, above W.P. landing.
Fort Putnam, 596 ft high, overlooks the river on the west side.
West Point Hotel has a fine look off to the N.
Constitution Island, opposite the Point.
Old Cro' Nest. On W side, above the Point.
Cold Spring. On E bank, opposite Old Cro' Nest.
Undercliff. A short distance north of Cold Spring, once the house of Geo. P. Morris, on an elevated plateau above the river.
Mount Taurus, or Bull Hill above Undercliff.
Little Stony Point. Under Mt. Taurus. Named from resemblance to Stony Point, south of the Highlands.
Break Neck. Above Mount Taurus, on the E side.
Storm King. On W bank, above Old Cro' Nest.
Beacon Hill, seen on E bank above Break Neck.
Fishkill Mts. trend off to the NE, across the southern part of Dutchess County.

[illegible]
Hudson.
Washington's Headquarters, Newburgh, 1781-1783, seen as the boat approaches the city; an old building with tall chimneys and steep roof almost sloping to the foundation. A flagstaff marks the point.
Newburgh, 59 miles from New York.
Fishkill Landing. On the E side, ~~4 miles above Fishkill,~~ opposite Newburgh.
Low Point, or Carthage. On east side, 4 miles above Fishkill.
Devil's Danz Kammer; point on west bank covered with cedars. Hendrick Hudson here witnessed an Indian Pow Wow.
New Hamburgh, above Low Point, on the E side, at the mouth of Wappingers Creek.
Hampton Point, opposite New Hamburgh. Here are the finest white cedars on the river.
Irving Grinnell's Residence "Netherwood," just distinguished thru the trees near the River [illegible]
"The Cedars." Residence and grounds of Mr. James Lennox Banks, with high tower, seen for many miles north and south.
[illegible] Place, just north. The house was burned several years ago and never re-built.
Shawangunk Mountains, on the W side, [illegible] away in the distance toward the Catskills.
[illegible] and Milton, two pl[illegible] villages on the west bank.

nifies Barren Rock.
Vassar Brewery. Long white buildings above the landing.
New Paltz Landing, opposite Poughkeepsie.
Poughkeepsie, 74 miles from New York.
The Poughkeepsie Bridge.
F. J. Allen's Residence, with tower and beautiful grounds N of Rosehill.
College Hill Building, Parthenon style of architecture, once a school.
Poughkeepsie Water Works. The water is forced from Reservoirs near the river to a large Reservoir on College Hill.
Hudson River State Hospital. On the Hyde Park road. Large red Building.
Hyde Park, on the E side, six miles north of Poughkeepsie. Connected with Poughkeepsie by a succession of villas.
Walter Langdon's Residence, Mrs. Kirkpatrick's and W. F. Rogers'are north of Hyde Park, on east side.
Manresa Institute, large building above Crum Elbow on West side.
[illegible] Estate, above Manresa Institute, square house with square tower.
A. R. Frothingham. Grecian Portico with columns.
John Burroughs brown stone cottage, N of Frothingham"s.
Alexander Holland's Residence, formerly residence of John Jacob Astor, West bank.

to the north west.

The Hotel Kaaterskill and Catskill House can also be seen from this point, fifteen miles north of the Overlook.

William B. Dinsmoore's Residence, a large yellow building on Dinsmore's Point; one of the finest on the Hudson. The first house south of Mr. Dinsmore's on the E bank is Mathew Livingstone's; the second, Mrs. Hoyt's house, with French roof; the next, one-eight of a mile south, MR. J. Lawrence Lee's.

Windcliff, Residence of Mr. Fricke, on E bank; A large stone villa with central tower. it was formerly the estate of Edw. R. Jones. The residence just below belongs to MR. Jacob Rupert.

Ellerslie, Residence of Ex-Vice President, Levi P. Morton, below Rhinecliff.

Rhinecliff, or Rhinebeck Landing, on the E side.

City of Kingston, embraces Kingston and Rondout.

Old Beekman Place. As the steamer leaves Rhinebeck Landing, the old Beekman Place can be seen in the trees, ashort distance above the landing, one of the old Revolutionary houses.

Ferncliff, Residence of William Astor. Fine villa with pointed tower.

Garretson Place, N of Ferncliff, on E bank. This place, long known as Clifton Point, is now the property of Louis Ehler.

Cruger's Residence, on Cruger's Island, once called Lower Red Hook Island.
The First Steamboat, the Clermong, was built by Robert Fulton in the Cove, known as North Bay, just N of Cruger's Island.
Tivoli, on E side, 100 miles from New York.
Chateau of Tivoli, Residence of Col. Johnson L. De Peyster. French roof house on terrace south of Tivoli Station.
Glasco. South of Tivoli on W side.
Rose Hill, Residence of Gen. J. Watts de Peyster, E. side. Residence seen among the trees north of Tivoli Station.
Saugerties, on W side. A dock 3,600 feet long shows the enterprise of this village.
Idele, property of Miss Clarkson, known as the Old Chancellor Place.
Malden. Above Saugerties, on west side.
Clermont. Above Tivoli, on east side.
West Camp, on west side, above Malden.
Germantown, on E side 103 miles from New York.
Man in the Mountain. Between Germantown and Catskill we get a fine view of the reclining giant.
Burden Mines, on E bank, 1 mi S of Catskill Sta.
Herman Livingston's Residence, on point above.
Catskill Creek empties in to the Hudson south of Catskill Dock.
Catskill, 110 mi from N.Y. Village one mile W from landing. Route from this point to Catskill Mts. via Catskill Mt. R.R. and Otis Elevating Railway.

PIERMONT

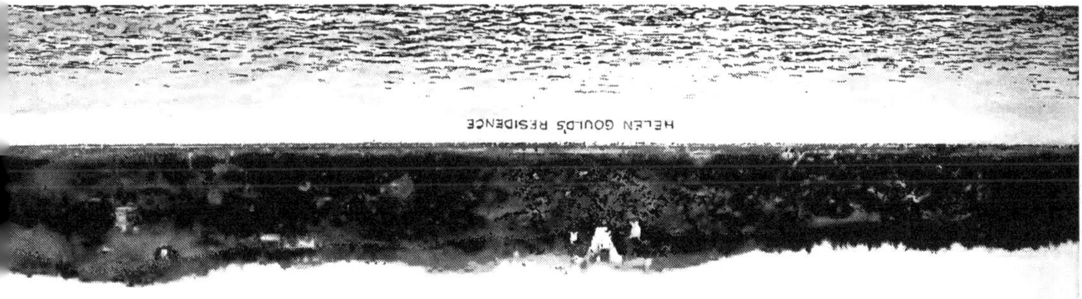

HELEN GOULD'S RESIDENCE

NYACK

TARRYTOWN

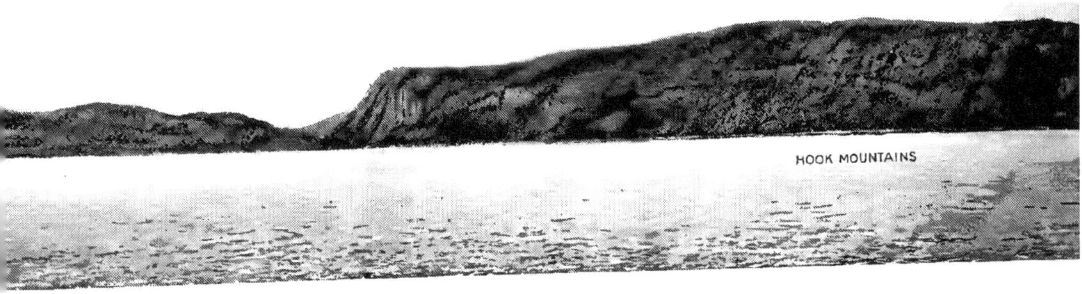
HOOK MOUNTAINS

SCARBOROUGH
MRS ELLIOTT F. SHEPPARD'S RESIDENCE
"ROCKWOOD" WILLIAM ROCKEFELLER'S RESIDENCE

AND LAKE.
POINT NO PO

PRISON BUILDINGS
SING SING VILLAGE.

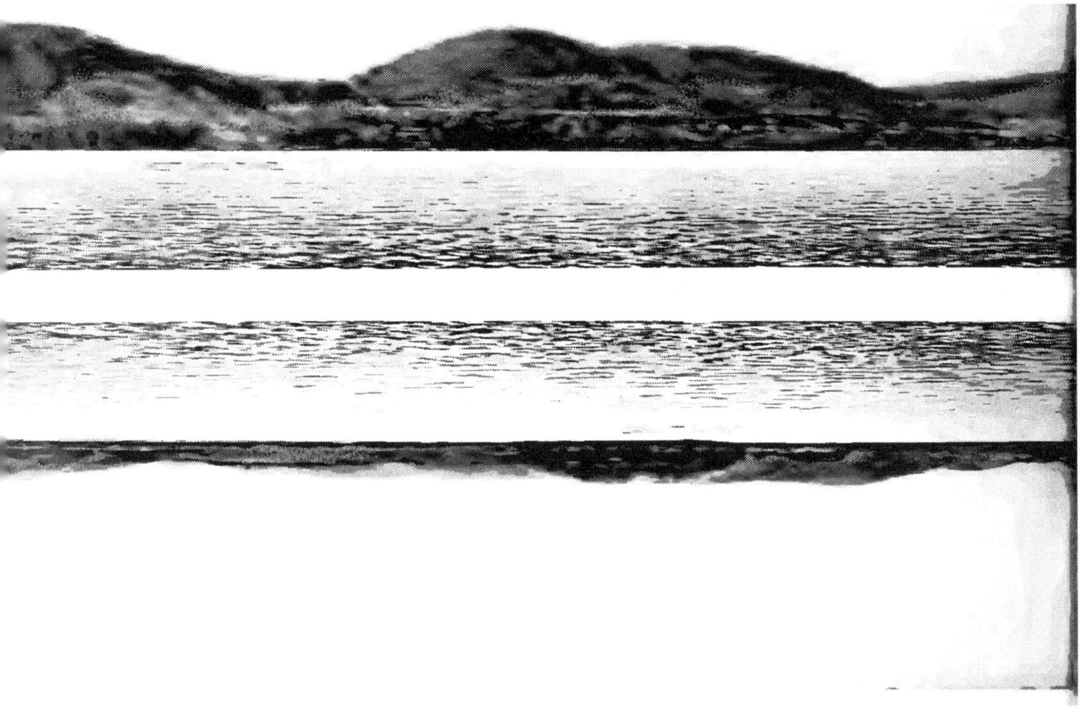

GRASSY POINT

VERPLANKS POINT

POINT.
TOMPKINS COVE.
DUNDERBERG MT.

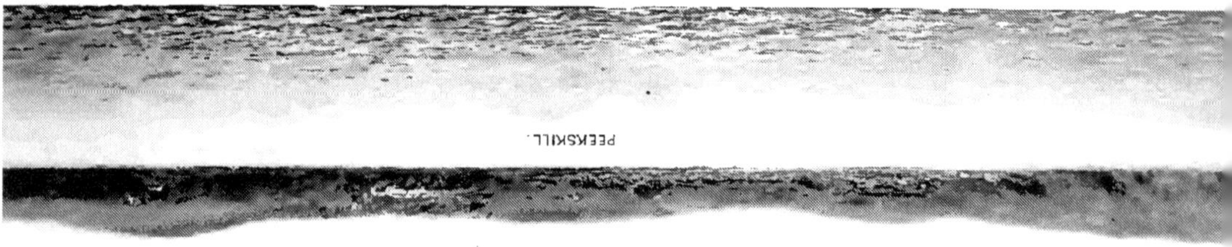
PEEKSKILL.

MANITO MT
NEW YORK STATE NATIONAL GUARD ENCAMPMENT

KIDD'S POIN

IONA ISLAND, GOVERNMENT GROUND
BEAR HILL. 1350

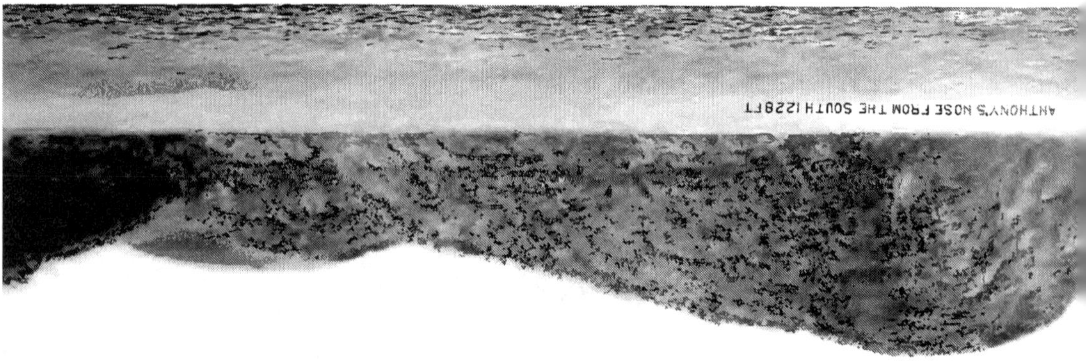
ANTHONY'S NOSE FROM THE SOUTH 1228 FT

FORT MONTGOMERY

ANTHONY'S NOSE FROM THE NORTH

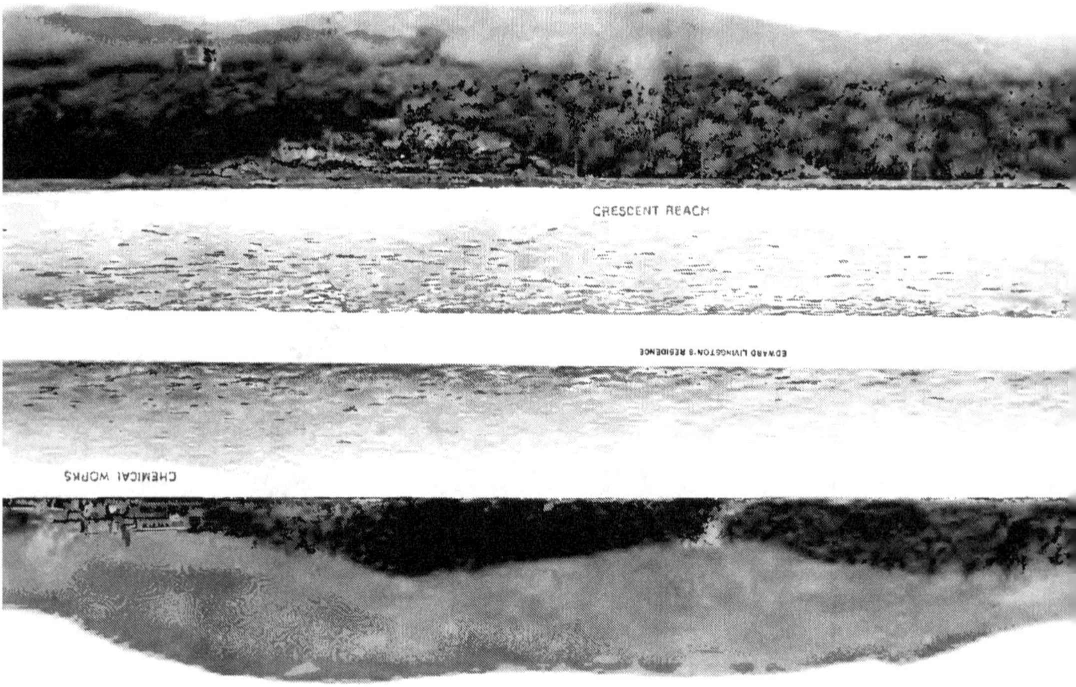

CRESCENT REACH
EDWARD LIVINGSTON'S RESIDENCE
CHEMICAL WORKS

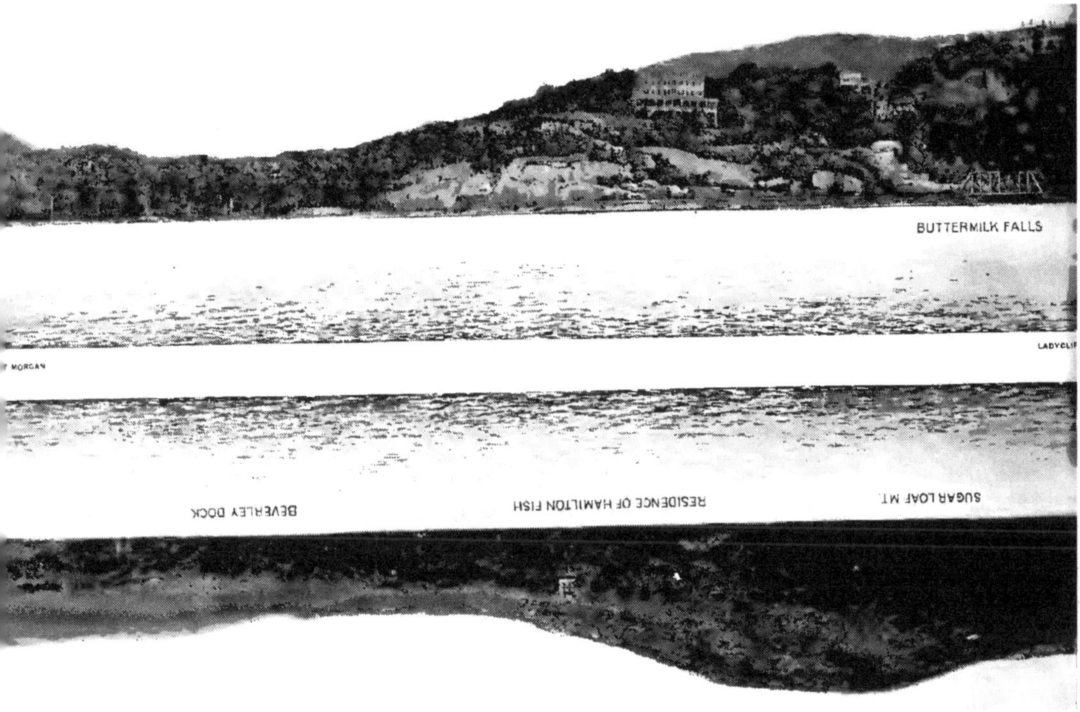
BUTTERMILK FALLS
LADYCLIF
MORGAN
SUGAR LOAF MT.
RESIDENCE OF HAMILTON FISH
BEVERLEY DOCK

HIGHLAND FALLS

WEST POINT MILITARY ACADEMY
DADE'S MONUMENT
CONSTITUTION POINT

BATTLE MONUMENT
BARRACKS
WEST POINT

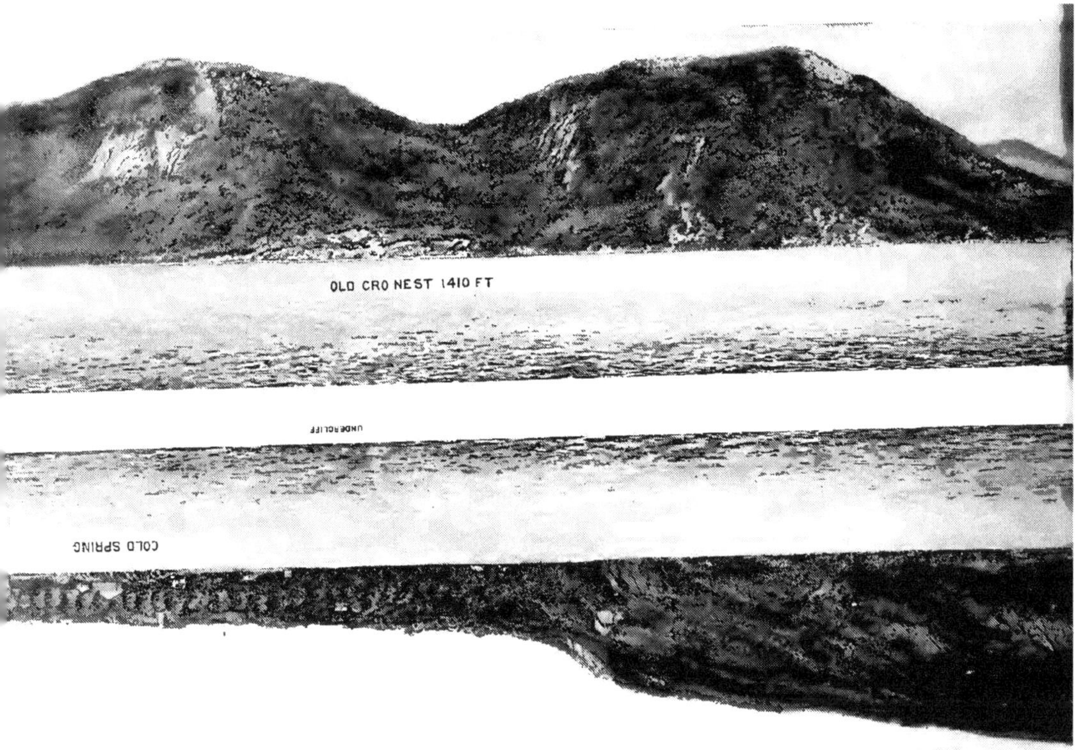
OLD CRO NEST 1410 FT
UNDERCLIFF
COLD SPRING

BEACON MTS
BREAKN

WASHINGTON'S HEADQUARTERS
MT BEACON INCLINE RAILROAD
DENNING'S

BURGH

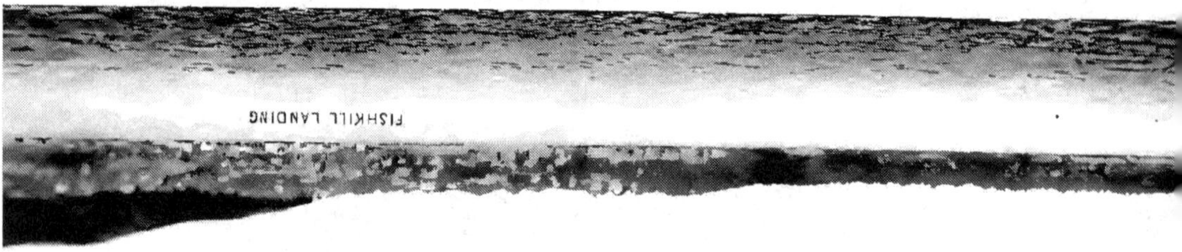
FISHKILL LANDING

ROSETON

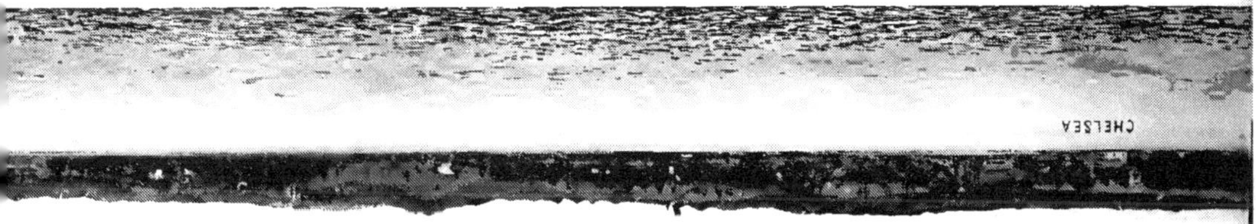
CHELSEA

DANSKAMMER

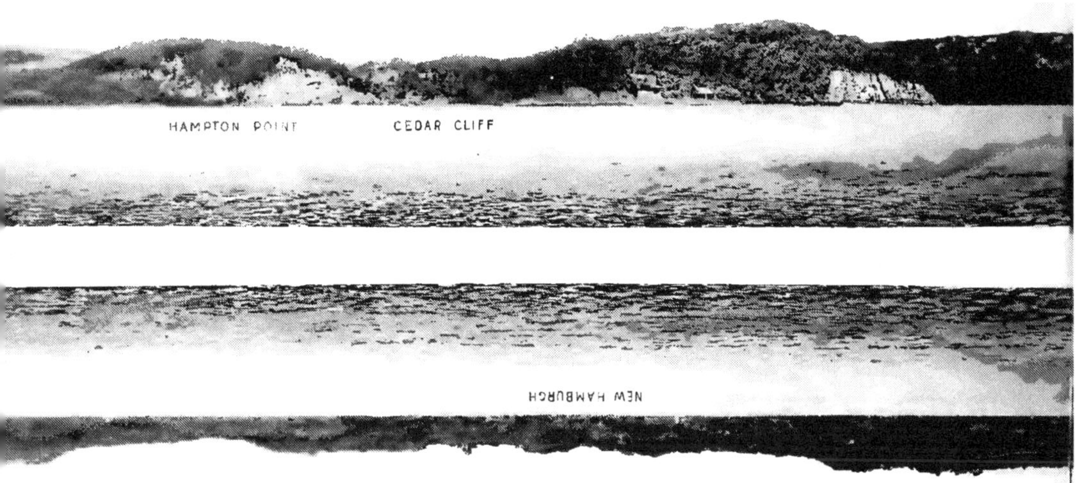
HAMPTON POINT
CEDAR CLIFF
NEW HAMBURGH

OROUGH

CLINTON PO
CAMELOT

MILTON

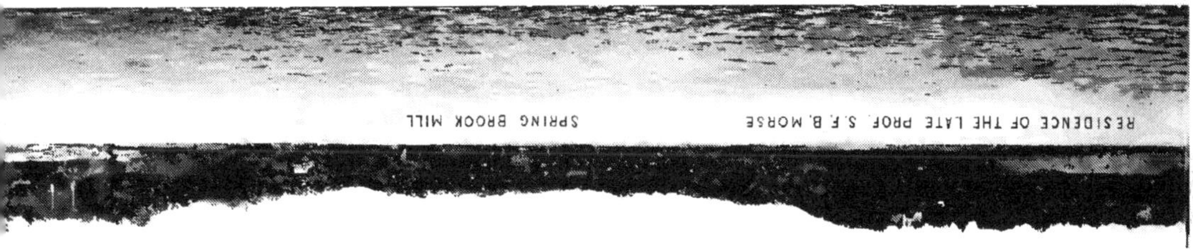
RESIDENCE OF THE LATE PROF. S. F. B. MORSE
SPRING BROOK MILL

BLUE POINT

KAAL ROCK
VASSAR HOSPITAL
LOVERS'

POUGHKEEPSIE
DAY LI

LANDING

POUGHKEEPSIE PUMPING STATION
HUDSON RIVER STATE HOSPITAL
COLLEGE

KRUM ELBOW

RESIDENCE OF A. ROGERS

MONASTERY OF

...IDENCE OF FREDERICK W. VANDERBILT

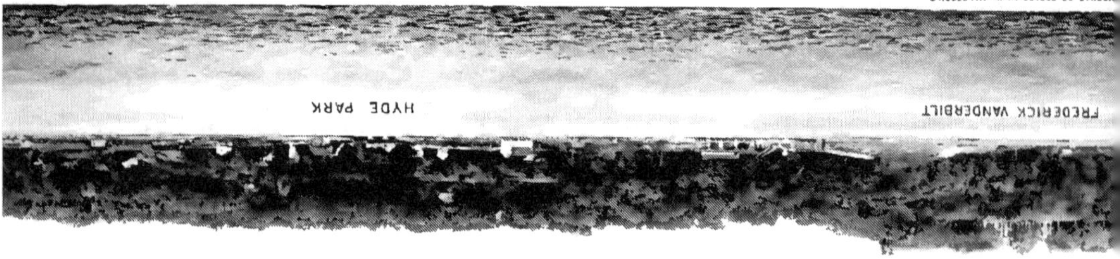

RESIDENCE OF ALTON B. PARKER

ESOPUS LIGHT-HOUSE

RESIDENCE OF LATE WM B DINSMORE
D.O. MILLS

RESIDENCE OF

PORT EWEN

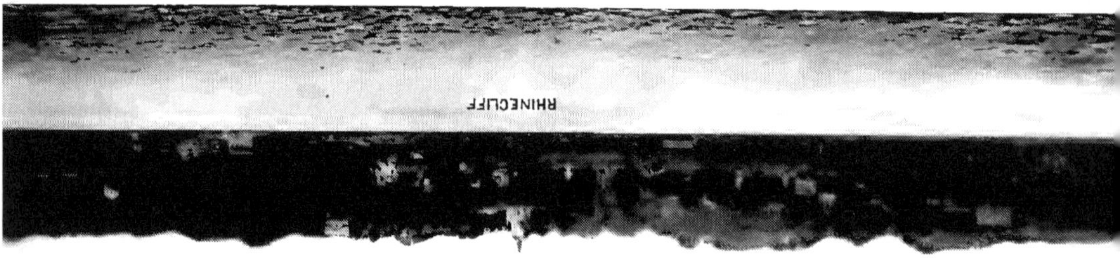
RHINECLIFF

(CITY OF KINGSTON)
KINGSTON POINT

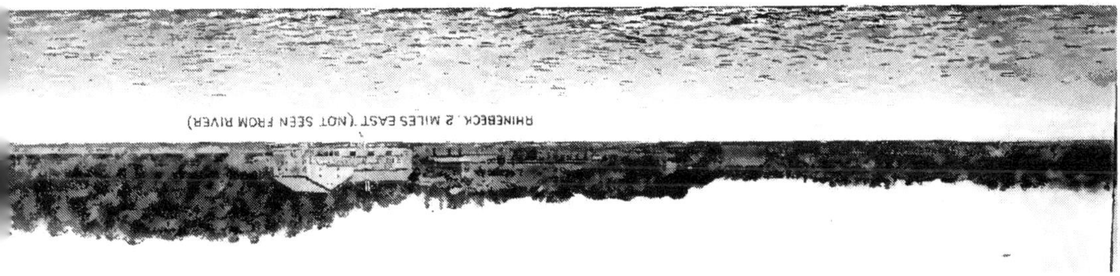
RHINEBECK, 2 MILES EAST (NOT SEEN FROM RIVER)

CLIFTON POINT

FLATBUSH

WILLIAM ASTOR'S RESIDENCE

TURKEY POINT

BARRYTOWN   DONALDSON

CRUGER'S ISLAND

MONTGOMERY PLACE

GLASCO

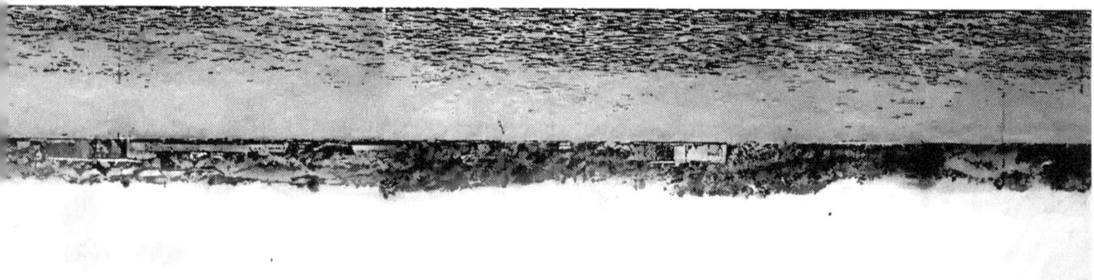

100 MILES FROM N. Y.

OVERLOOK MT.

TIVOLI (100 M FROM N. Y.)

SAUGERTIES SAUGERTIES LIGHT-HOUSE

GEN'L J. W. DePEYSTER'S RESIDENCE

KAATERSKILL HIGH PEAK HOTEL KAATERSKILL MALDEN CATSKILL MT. HOUSE

LIVINGSTON RESIDENCE

EVESPORT

LIVINGSTON'S FLATS

WEST CAMP

GERMANTOWN

KNEE
BREAST
HEAD
OVER REACH
MAN IN THE MOUNTAIN
THE CATSKILLS
110 MILES FROM N. Y.

GERMANTOWN STATION
GERMANTOWN LANDING
ANSEN'S CREEK

"HALF MOON," HENDRICK HUDSON, SEPT. 16, 1609

CATSKILL (111 M FROM

LIVINGSTON'S DOCK

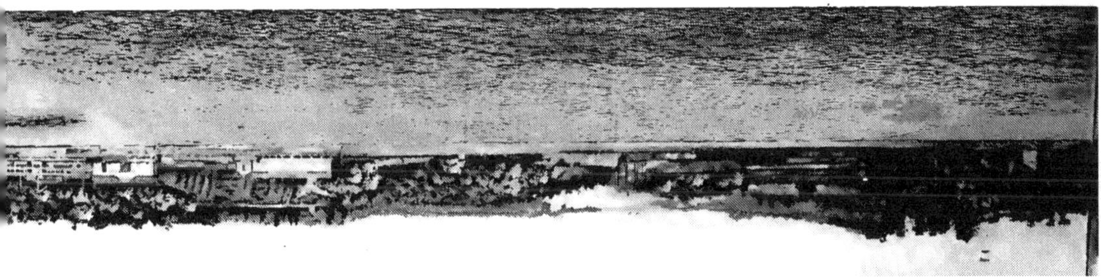

PROSPECT PARK HOTEL

GREENDALE

COLE'S GROVE

F. S. CHURCH'S RESIDENCE

S ISLAND

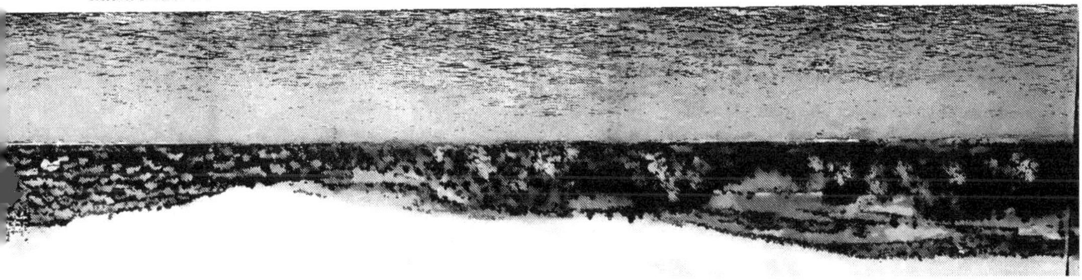

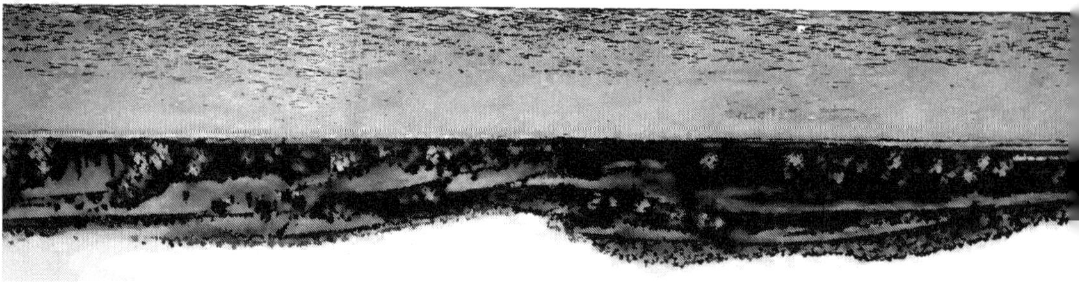

MOUNT MERINO

HUDSON FLATS

HUDSON FROM THE SOUTH

HUDSON LIGHT-HOUSE

STATE REFORMATORY

ATHENS — HUDSON F

HUDSON (115 M FROM N.Y.) — PROMENADE HILL

THE BECKER REACH

NORTH BAY

123 MILES FROM N. Y.

DU BOIS RESIDENCE

FOUR MILE-POINT LIGHT-HOUSE

STOCKPORT STATION

KINDERHOOK CREEK

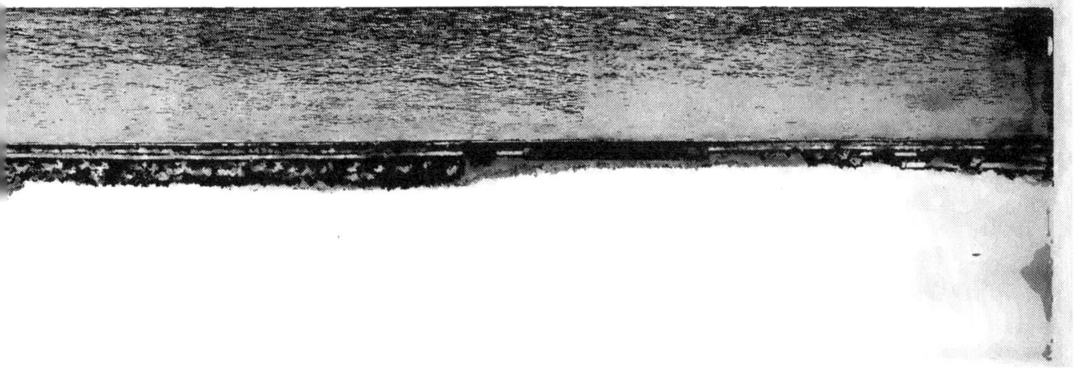

ICE HOUSES

STOCKPORT LANDING

COXSACKIE

COXSACKIE FERRY

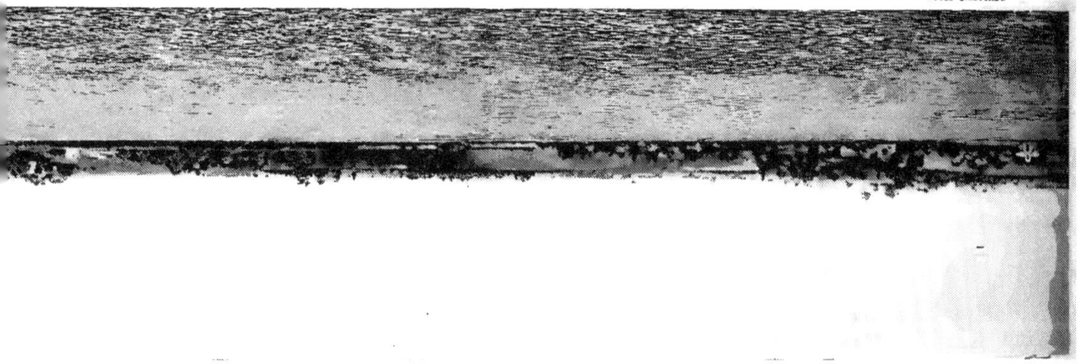

COXSACKIE (128 M FROM N. Y.)

PROSPECT GROVE

COXSACKIE LIGHT-HOUSE

STUYVESANT LANDING

128 MILES FROM N. Y.

STUYVESANT STATION

COXSACKIE CREEK

STUYVESANT LIGHT-HOUSE

130 MILES FROM N. Y.

ISLAND BEACHES

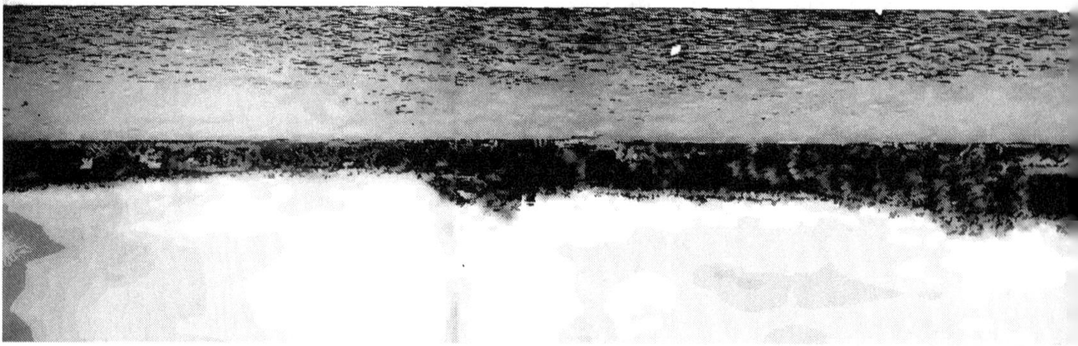

NEW BALTIMORE (131 M FROM N. Y.)

ISLAND REACHES

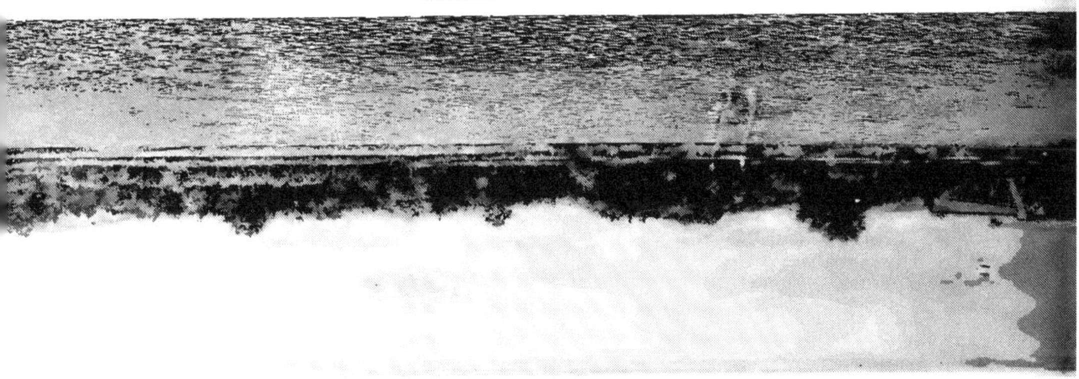

BEERY ISLAND

MEETING POINT OF FOUR COUNTIES: COLUMBIA, RENSSELAER, GREENE AND ALBANY

COEYMANS

LOWER SCHODACK ISLAND

TENEYCK BROOK'S RESIDENCE

SCHODACK ISLAND

CASTLETON

CEDAR HILL

SUNNYSIDE ISLAND

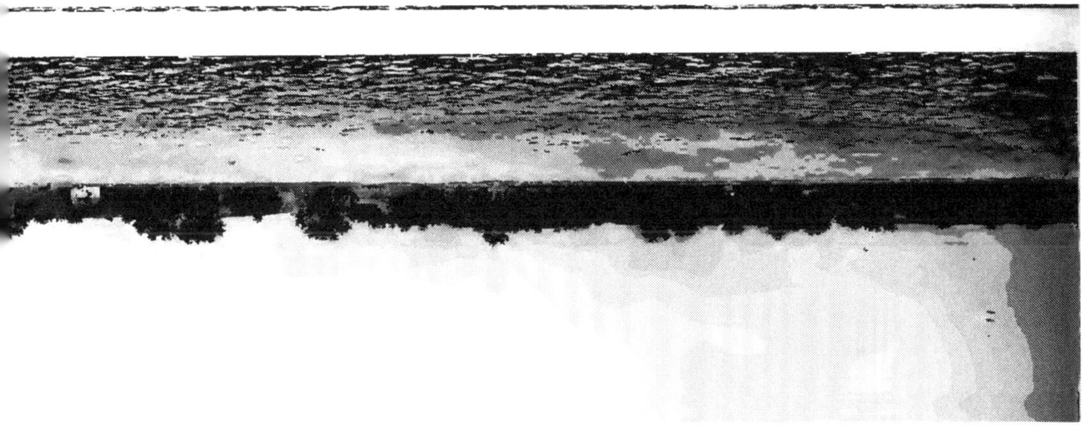

PARDA HOOK

STAATS ISLAND

OVERSLAUGH BAR

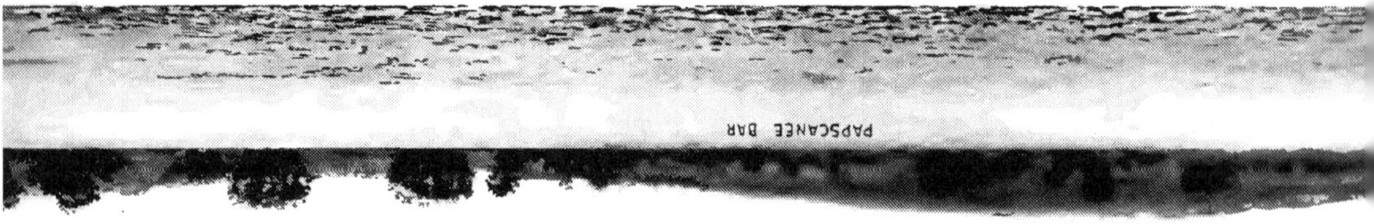
PAPSCANEE BAR

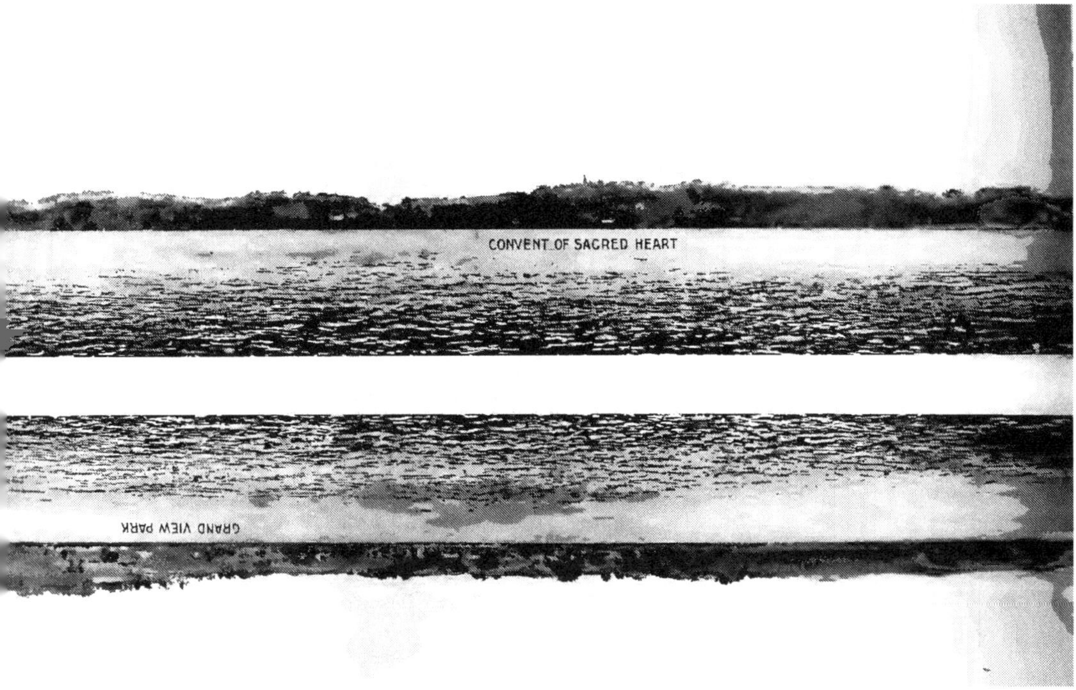
CONVENT OF SACRED HEART
GRAND VIEW PARK

ALBANY

DOW'S POINT
RENSSELAER
ENSSELAER PLACE 1642

ALBANY
RENSSELAER

ALBANY
STATE CAPITOL
RENSSELAER